Ideas for Special Days

Easy-to-do Activities for Ages 3 - 12

Publisher ....*Arthur L. Miley*

Author ....*Nancy Williamson*

Managing Editor ....*Carol Rogers*

Assistant Editor ....*Chris D. Neynaber*

Art Director ....*Deborah Birch*

Illustrator ....*Roger Johnson*

Cover Illustrator ....*Court Patton*

Proofreader ....*Heather Swindle*

Rainbow Books

Copyright 1996 • Fifth Printing
Rainbow Books • P.O. Box 261129 • San Diego, CA 92196

#RB36108
ISBN 0-937282-01-4

Thou wilt show me the path of life:
in Thy presence is fulness of joy;
at Thy right hand there are pleasures for evermore.

— Psalm 16:11

Ideas for Special Days

Easy-to-do Activities for Ages 3 - 12

Introduction

Special days provide very exciting opportunities for teaching God's precepts to children in a fun, relaxed atmosphere. New Year's Day, for example, is a time when we all resolve to do better; therefore, this holiday is an excellent time to encourage young Christians to *"press toward the mark for the prize of the high calling of God in Christ Jesus"* (Philippians 3:14). Of course, Valentine's Day is a tremendous occasion to emphasize God's love and His commandment to us to love one another. At Easter we learn about forgiveness and new life in Christ.

Unfortunately, the world has taken nearly all of these Christian holidays (holy-days) and prostituted their meanings. Commercialization and secularization have corrupted these special days and have turned them into festivals celebrating anything but the love of God and His plan of redemption and eternal life. As worldly values infiltrate the celebration of our holidays, even some of our churches have begun to propagate these secularized festivals. The origins of our Christian holidays are becoming increasingly obscure to today's youth.

In order to teach children the Christian roots of our national holidays, we must reemphasize the reasons for these special times and holy days and present Christ-centered ways to celebrate. Because Christianity is a never-ending celebration of God's love for each person, every day of the year should give cause to celebrate in ways that will both be pleasing to God and beneficial to His people.

52 Ideas for Special Days will fill your calendar with plans, projects, and parties for many special occasions throughout the year. In this book you will find ideas for commemorating national legal holidays that will help restore and nurture patriotism and pride in our country. You will learn ways to celebrate church holy days that will teach children about God's love, grace, and will for their lives. This book also provides ideas for observing the passing of the four seasons which demonstrate the creative wisdom of God while instructing children in ways to enjoy and protect the environment that God gave us. Also included are ideas for such special days as birthdays and vacations. Even Christianity's Jewish heritage is highlighted by teaching how to commemorate Hanukkah, one of the special days that Jesus celebrated when He walked this earth.

The main purpose of *52 Ideas for Special Days* is to remind each of us that God created us and provided for our salvation through His Son, Jesus Christ. Whenever we are mindful of God during the special days we celebrate, we are giving God the glory for the blessings He has bestowed upon us. It is our prayer that by observing Christ-centered celebrations, our children will become firmly rooted in Christian principles and desire to live lives that will be pleasing to God.

Calendar and Scripture Index

JANUARY
January 1 • **New Year's Day**
Spiritual Inventory *(Jeremiah 26:13)* 7
January 6 • **Epiphany**
What Can I Give Him? *(Psalm 116:12)* 8

FEBRUARY
February 14 • **Valentine's Day**
Pass the Hearts Game *(I Thessalonians 3:12)* 9
Showing God's Love *(John 15:12)* 10
Third Monday in February • **Presidents' Day**
Following Honest Leaders *(Philippians 4:8)* 11

MARCH—APRIL
March 17 • **St. Patrick's Day**
Help St. Patrick Teach *(II Peter 3:18)* 12
Sunday before Easter • **Palm Sunday**
Triumphal Entry *(John 12:32)* 13
Friday before Easter • **Good Friday**
King of the Jews *(Matthew 27:35)* 15
Between March 22 and April 25 • **Easter**
Easter Object Lesson *(Matthew 28:7)* 16
An Easter Newspaper *(Mark 16:15)* 17
Easter Crosses *(Mark 16:6)* 17
New Life *(I Corinthians 15:44)* 18
Easter Lilies *(Luke 24:6)* 18
An Easter Acrostic *(Luke 24:7)* 19
Seventh Sunday after Easter • **Pentecost**
Praise Festival *(Acts 1:8)* 20

MAY
May 5 • **Children's Day**
This Is What I Can Do *(Proverbs 8:32)* 21
First Thursday in May • **National Day of Prayer**
Follow-the-Leader Prayer *(Psalm 5:2)* 22
Second Sunday in May • **Mother's Day**
Bible Mothers Quiz *(Ephesians 6:1)* 23
Mother's Day Coupon Book *(Prov. 31:30)* 24
Giant Mother's Day Card *(Ephesians 6:2-3)* 24
Last Monday in May • **Memorial Day**
Giving All in Love *(John 15:13)* 25

JUNE—JULY
June 14 • **Flag Day**
Happy Birthday, Old Glory *(Psalm 20:5)* 26
Third Sunday in June • **Father's Day**
Bible Fathers Quiz *(Ephesians 6:1-2)* 27
Father's Day Card *(Proverbs 10:1)* 28
Dad's Car Bag *(Ephesians 6:2)* 28
July 4 • **Independence Day**
God and Country *(John 8:36)* 29

AUGUST—SEPTEMBER
August or September • **Promotion Day**
Graduation *(I Peter 2:2)* 30
First Monday in September • **Labor Day**
A Mind to Work *(II Thessalonians 3:10)* 31
September • **Back to School**
Homecoming *(Galatians 3:26)* 32
Second Sunday in September • **Grandparent's Day**
Grandparents Join the Class *(Proverbs 5:1)* 33

OCTOBER
October 12 • **Columbus Day**
Overcoming Difficulties *(II Timothy 4:17)* 34
Oct. 31 • **Harvest Festival (Halloween Alternatives)**
Turn-About Treats *(Matthew 10:8)* 36
Paper Bag Costume Party *(Romans 12:21)* 37

NOVEMBER
Fourth Thursday in November • **Thanksgiving**
Paper Bag Pilgrims and Indians *(Psalm 92:1)* 38
Thanksgiving Notes *(Psalm 136:1)* 41
Thanksgiving Fun *(Psalm 35:9)* 43
The four weeks before Christmas • **Advent**
Family Advent Wreath *(Matthew 1:23)* 44
Advent Giving Tree *(Acts 20:35)* 45
Advent Bulletin Board *(Matthew 1:21)* 47

DECEMBER
December • **Hanukkah**
Dreidel Game *(Luke 2:52)* 48
December 25 • **Christmas**
Christmas Wreath *(Isaiah 9:6)* 49
Christmas Plan-Ahead Program *(Luke 2:7)* 51
Christmas Tree Puzzle *(Luke 2:11)* 52
Little Children's Tree *(Matthew 2:2)* 53
Christmas Fun *(Luke 2:14)* 54

OTHER CELEBRATED DAYS
Birthdays
Happy Birthday! *(Psalm 107:15)* 55
Summer • June-August
Summer Clean-Up Picnic *(Proverbs 10:5)* 56
Fall • September-November
Fall Mobile *(Ecclesiastes 3:1)* 57
Winter • December-February
Snowy Landscape Picture *(Ecclesiastes 3:11)* 59
Spring • March-May
Spring Fling *(Psalm 118:24)* 60
Vacation Time
My Travel Book *(Jude 21)* 61
Year 'Round
Make It Through the Year Game
(Ecclesiastes 3:1) 62

Table of Contents

1 New Year's Day
Spiritual Inventory 7

2 Epiphany
What Can I Give Him? 8

3 Valentine's Day
Pass the Hearts Game 9

4 Valentine's Day
Showing God's Love 10

5 Presidents' Day
Following Honest Leaders 11

6 St. Patrick's Day
Help St. Patrick Teach 12

7 Palm Sunday
Triumphal Entry 13

8 Good Friday
King of the Jews 15

9 Easter
Easter Object Lesson 16

10 Easter
An Easter Newspaper 17

11 Easter
Easter Crosses 17

12 Easter
New Life 18

13 Easter
Easter Lilies 18

14 Easter
An Easter Acrostic 19

15 Pentecost
Praise Festival 20

16 Children's Day
This Is What I Can Do 21

17 National Day of Prayer
Follow-the-Leader Prayer 22

18 Mother's Day
Bible Mothers Quiz 23

19 Mother's Day
Mother's Day Coupon Book 24

20 Mother's Day
Giant Mother's Day Card 24

21 Memorial Day
Giving All in Love 25

22 Flag Day
Happy Birthday, Old Glory 26

23 Father's Day
Bible Fathers Quiz 27

24 Father's Day
Father's Day Card 28

25 Father's Day
Dad's Car Bag 28

26 Independence Day
God and Country 29

27 Promotion Day
Graduation 30

28 Labor Day
A Mind to Work 31

29 Back to School
Homecoming 32

30 Grandparent's Day
Grandparents Join the Class 33

31 Columbus Day
Overcoming Difficulties 34

32 Harvest Festival (Halloween Alternatives)
Turn-About Treats 36

33 Harvest Festival (Halloween Alternatives)
Paper Bag Costume Party 37

34 Thanksgiving
Paper Bag Pilgrims and Indians 38

35 Thanksgiving
Thanksgiving Notes 41

36 Thanksgiving
Thanksgiving Fun 43

37 Advent
Family Advent Wreath 44

38 Advent
Advent Giving Tree 45

39 Advent
Advent Bulletin Board 47

40 Hanukkah
Dreidel Game 48

41 Christmas
Christmas Wreath 49

42 Christmas
Christmas Plan-Ahead Program 51

43 Christmas
Christmas Tree Puzzle 52

44 Christmas
Little Children's Tree 53

45 Christmas
Christmas Fun 54

46 Birthdays
Happy Birthday! 55

47 Summer
Summer Clean-Up Picnic 56

48 Fall
Fall Mobile 57

49 Winter
Snowy Landscape Picture 59

50 Spring
Spring Fling 60

51 Vacation Time
My Travel Book 61

52 Year 'Round
Make It Through the Year Game 62

New Year's Day — January 1

The beginning of a new year is an excellent time for children to resolve to live Christlike lives. At the beginning of each new year businesses take inventory of the stock they have; this helps them to know how much money or progress they made during the past year and how much they have to purchase or produce for the next year. People need to take a spiritual inventory at the beginning of each new year in order to see what elements of their lives they need to improve. Then they can make resolutions, or promises to themselves, to do things differently in the new year.

1 New Year's Day
Spiritual Inventory

OBJECTIVE: To encourage children to inventory their lives and set new Christian-living goals

Appropriate for ages 6 to 12

"Therefore now amend your ways and your doings, and obey the voice of the Lord your God."
— Jeremiah 26:13

Suggest that the boys and girls take a spiritual inventory of their own lives to see how they can improve in this new year. Pass out sheets of paper with the following questions, or write the questions on the chalkboard. Allow time for each child to answer all the questions, and then discuss the answers.

After this discussion, ask the children to make spiritual resolutions and write down one or more things they intend to do better or differently in the new year. Give each child an envelope and write his or her name on the front. Seal the children's spiritual resolutions inside their envelopes. Collect the envelopes and keep them until late in the year (or the beginning of the next new year). At that time, give the envelopes back to the children so they can check to see if they have achieved the goals they set.

Close this session with prayer, asking Jesus to help each boy and girl to live closer to Him, and to be able to accomplish the goals they have set.

Spiritual Inventory Questions:
1. Do I pray every day?
2. Do I read my Bible daily?
3. Do I attend church as well as Sunday school?
4. Do I give a part of my allowance to the Lord's work?
5. Do I really love all people everywhere?
6. Do I treat others as I would have them treat me?
7. Do I respect my parents and teachers?
8. Am I a good citizen?
9. Do I do my lessons honestly in school?
10. Have I confessed Christ before others? If not, will I receive Christ and witness daily this year?

Epiphany — January 6

Epiphany (Three Kings Day) is celebrated by many Hispanic children. It is a time to remember the journey of the Magi, the wise men (legend names them Caspar, Melchior, and Balthazar) to the birthplace of the baby Jesus. The wise men brought gifts of gold, frankincense, and myrrh to the young child Jesus. On the night before Three Kings Day, children fill boxes with grass or straw. This grass is for the kings' camels. The children then place these boxes under their beds, in hopes that the kings will leave gifts in place of the grass or straw.

2 Epiphany
What Can I Give Him?

OBJECTIVE: To encourage children to give their gifts of life and love to Jesus

Appropriate for ages 4 to 9

"What shall I render unto the LORD for all His benefits toward me?"
— Psalm 116:12

This special day gives children the opportunity to think about what gifts they can give Jesus. He is no longer a baby in a manger, but He grew up, gave His life so that we would not have to pay the penalty for our sins, rose from the dead, and now lives in Heaven with God, His Father. Jesus wants to receive gifts from us today. He wants us to love Him, to talk with Him, to obey Him, and to read God's Word.

Provide a shoe box or other small box for each child. Also supply some straw or Easter basket grass, and let the children fill their boxes with it. Then have each child write or draw on a piece of paper what they would like to give to Jesus during this new year and place their "gift" in the box. The boxes can be taken home to be put in the child's room as a reminder of what he or she wants to give Jesus.

Valentine's Day — February 14

St. Valentine's Day is a wonderful opportunity to help children think lovingly about those who make their lives better, such as parents, relatives, friends, teachers, workers in the church, police officers, and other public servants. It also provides an excellent time to help children understand Christ's commission to love one another (John 15:12).

Allow time on Valentine Sunday for children to talk about ways in which they can show love to others...not just on this day but every day of the year.

---

3 Valentine's Day
Pass the Hearts Game

OBJECTIVE: To teach children that they can enjoy learning to love one another

Appropriate for ages 3 to 12

*"May the Lord make your love increase and overflow
for each other and for everyone else,
just as ours does for you."*
— I Thessalonians 3:12 (NIV)

Players make a large circle around the leader. The teacher selects one child to start the game. This child will hold a securely-tied bag of Valentine heart candy. As the children pass the bag of candy from player to player, the leader will sing the following lyrics to the tune of WHERE, OH WHERE HAS MY LITTLE DOG GONE:

Where, oh where has the candy gone?
Oh where, oh where can it be?
With the bag tied tight for the party tonight,
Oh where, oh where can it be?

The leader should stop singing unexpectedly in the middle of a line or word. Whoever is holding the bag of candy when the singing stops must go into the circle with the leader. This continues until only one child is not standing with the leader; this child is the winner. When the game is over, the candy can be shared by all of the players, with the winner having first choice.

4 Valentine's Day
Showing God's Love

OBJECTIVE: To help children think lovingly about others

Appropriate for ages 3 to 12

"This is My commandment, That ye love one another, as I have loved you."
— John 15:12

The week before Valentine's Day let the children prepare a special Valentine Week family devotion packet. Duplicate the large heart pattern and the small heart pattern onto red construction paper so that each child has two large hearts and seven small hearts. Let the children cut out their red paper hearts. (Cut out the hearts ahead of time for very young children.) Then let the children glue the sides and bottom tip of the large hearts together, leaving the top open to make an envelope.

Write the scripture references listed below on the seven small hearts, one reference per heart. Then place these smaller hearts inside the large heart envelope. Instruct the children to take one small Bible reference heart from the large heart envelope each day at home during Valentine Week, and read it as part of family devotions.

Scripture References:
John 13:34
John 15:10
John 14:23-24
John 13:35
John 15:12
Romans 8:28
Psalm 18:1-2

Completed Envelope

Large Heart

Small Heart

Presidents' Day — Third Monday in February

Presidents' Day is a commemoration of the birthdays of two of the greatest presidents in American history: George Washington (the first president) and Abraham Lincoln (the sixteenth president).

Both of these famous leaders were committed Christians, and both were known for their honesty and integrity. Therefore, it is fitting that this holiday be used as a means to teach children the value of honesty.

5 Presidents' Day
Following Honest Leaders

OBJECTIVE: To help children understand and apply the concept of honesty

Appropriate for ages 4 to 9

"Brethren, whatsoever things are true, whatsoever things are honest, whatsoever things are just . . . think on these things."
— Philippians 4:8

Plan a patriotic party that emphasizes the value of honesty. Send special red, white, and blue invitations to your class members a week before the party. Write the following on the invitation:

We're having a party,
    The theme's red, white, and blue,
We want you to come
    And bring your friends, too.

    Time: (whatever time Sunday school starts)
    Date: (the Sunday before Presidents' Day)
    Place: (wherever your class meets)

Provide a small American flag for each child (be sure to have extras for any visitors who may attend). You may wish to decorate the room with red, white, and blue balloons and crepe paper streamers. Serve refreshments such as white frosted cupcakes with red and blue sprinkles on top and red fruit punch.

To emphasize honesty, a money hunt will be a fun activity. Duplicate the silver dollar pattern below on grey construction paper. Reproduce the dollar bill pattern below on green construction paper. Hide an equal number of these coins and dollar bills around the room before the children arrive.

When you are ready to play the game, divide the players into two groups, the Washingtons and the Lincolns. The Washington group will look for the coins while the Lincoln group looks for the bills. Instruct the children to begin the search at the same time. The object will be to find as much money as possible in a given length of time. The members of the Washington group must ignore any bills they find and the Lincoln group must ignore any coins they find. The group finding the most money wins.

Along with your regular lesson for the day, tell a story about one or both of the great presidents whom we are honoring. Close with prayer, asking God to help each child to be a good, honest citizen.

St. Patrick's Day — March 17

On March 17 the Irish people honor St. Patrick, the patron saint of Ireland, who died on this date over 1500 years ago.

St. Patrick was known for his love of learning. Most people of his time were not educated, so St. Patrick taught all the people he baptized how to read and write. These skills are very important for those who wish to learn about God and His Word. Because the shamrock is the national flower of Ireland, it is an ancient custom to wear a shamrock or a bit of green on St. Patrick's Day in memory of St. Patrick.

6 St. Patrick's Day
Help St. Patrick Teach

OBJECTIVE: To demonstrate to children the importance of learning about God

Appropriate for ages 6 to 12

"But grow in grace, and in the knowledge of our Lord and Saviour Jesus Christ."
— II Peter 3:18

St. Patrick placed such a great value on education that he taught everyone he baptized how to read and write. We want children to know that we, also, are concerned about their education. Naturally we are most concerned that children learn the Word of God and use it as the foundation on which to build their lives.

Have the children make shamrocks out of green construction paper as a reminder to read their Bibles. Using the pattern below, have the children cut three hearts each and glue or tape them together to make a shamrock. Tape a green chenille wire on the shamrock for a stem. The children can then print the memory verse on one side of their shamrock and the words, READ THE BIBLE on the other side. Help them twist the chenille wire around a button or their wrist as a reminder to read their Bibles.

Shamrock Leaf Pattern

Palm Sunday — Sunday before Easter

In the story of the triumphant entry of Jesus into Jerusalem (Mark 11:1-10), we often forget something very important. We may be so busy thinking of the people who sang praises and spread their garments before the Lord, that we forget the little donkey that carried Him into the city. More is told about the donkey than about the people who sang.

7 Palm Sunday
Triumphal Entry

OBJECTIVE: To teach children to tell others about Christ so others can know Him

Appropriate for ages 4 to 12

"But I, when I am lifted up from the earth, will draw all men to Myself."
— John 12:32 (NIV)

In the Old Testament we are told that certain unclean animals could not be eaten. Donkeys were among those unclean animals. In Exodus 13:13 we are told that the first-born donkeys must be redeemed with a lamb, or the donkey's neck must be broken. Just as the lamb had to take the place of the donkey, so the Spotless Lamb, Jesus, had to die in the place of people whose lives are not clean. Everyone needs Christ, the Lamb of God, Who died for our sin.

Then, too, the donkey was used by Christ. The donkey carried the Saviour into the city. Jesus can use boys and girls, too. Whenever you see a donkey you will remember how the Lord Jesus refused to become a king in this sinful world in order that He might die on a cross to save us from our sins. The donkey could not talk, but it could lift Christ so others could see Him. God wants us to imitate this little donkey who helped to make Christ known as He entered the city of Jerusalem.

Duplicate the donkey pattern so that each child will have two copies. Let each child color the

donkeys gray or brown and then cut them out. Glue the two bodies together leaving the legs free. Spread apart the legs so the donkey will stand. Provide one copy of the palm leaf pattern for each child. Have them color it green and cut it out. Glue or tape the donkey's feet to the palm leaf. The children can place the little donkey in their room to remind them that they, too, can lift up Jesus by telling others about Him.

Good Friday — Friday before Easter

On the Friday before Easter we remember Jesus' death on the cross. Some churches hold a special noontime service on this day as a reminder of the suffering Jesus went though for our sakes.

This is a good time to help the children realize that Jesus died for them personally. Explain that Jesus did not stay dead, but He came alive again. We celebrate His resurrection on Easter.

8 Good Friday
King of the Jews

OBJECTIVE: To help children understand and appreciate that Jesus died for them

Appropriate for ages 6 to 9

"And they crucified Him, and parted His garments, casting lots."
— Matthew 27:35

Read Matthew 27:33-50 to the children, then give each child a copy of the following puzzle and a pencil, marker, or crayon. Explain that a title was put on the cross above Christ's head. It was written in Greek, Hebrew, and Latin.

The mysterious writing below will tell you what was on the sign. Complete the top of each letter to find out what the sign says. If you get stuck, the answer is in Matthew 27:37.

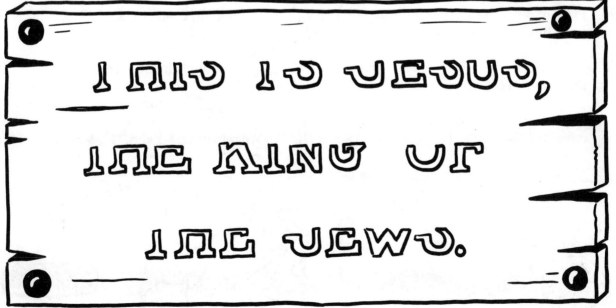

Easter — Between March 22 and April 25

Easter celebrates the resurrection of Christ. It is observed on the first Sunday following the full moon that occurs on or after March 21, or one week later if the full moon falls on Sunday.

After telling the story of Easter to your children give them an opportunity to tell it back to you. This is a good way to discover if the children have any false ideas that need to be corrected. It is also a way to help them understand what really happened on that glorious day.

9 Easter
Easter Object Lesson

OBJECTIVE: To help children understand and remember the Easter story and to reinforce that Jesus lives

Appropriate for ages 6 to 12

"Go quickly, and tell His disciples that He is risen from the dead."
— Matthew 28:7

Collect the following items. Hold them up one by one and let the children tell what the item represents.

1. Donkey: reminds us of Jesus' triumphal entry to Jerusalem.

2. Small purse or bag containing coins: Judas was paid with coins to betray Jesus.

3. Small rooster: Peter denied Jesus three times before the cock crowed.

4. Piece of rope: they bound Jesus' hands and led Him away.

5. Thorns from a rose bush or hawthorn bush: the crown of thorns on Jesus' head.

6. Small wooden cross: Jesus carried His own cross to Calvary.

7. Piece of sponge: they gave Jesus vinegar to drink.

8. Small box with dirt and stones: the rocks rent and the earth quaked.

9. Soldier: the centurion said, "Truly this is the Son of God."

10. Piece of white linen: Nicodemus and Joseph took Jesus' body down from the cross and placed it in the tomb.

11. Angel: the angel said, "He is not here, He is risen."

12. Cotton or angel hair: Jesus went to live with His Father in Heaven.

52 Ideas for Special Days

10 Easter
An Easter Newspaper

OBJECTIVE: To help children spread the Good News that Jesus rose from the dead

Appropriate for ages 5 to 12

"And He said unto them, Go ye into all the world, and preach the gospel to every creature."
— Mark 16:15

This project can involve every member of your Sunday school as an Easter outreach into the community. Ask every person to write an article, poem, song, story, puzzle, or draw a picture about Easter. Emphasize that the writings and artwork are to be Bible-related, not about bunnies and new clothes.

This work should be finished at least two weeks before Easter. Form a committee to review the material and lay it out in newspaper format. Contact a printer who will run your edition on regular newsprint and fold it like a newspaper or have it copied onto 11 x 17-inch paper and folded in half. The finished papers should be ready for distribution by Maundy Thursday (the day before Good Friday).

Be sure you have enough copies printed so that there will be one for each home in the area surrounding your church . . . and have extras to give out at special services. Ask volunteers to deliver the papers to homes in your church neighborhood. This project will provide an excellent opportunity for children to express their feelings about Easter and what Jesus did for them. It also will get the true message of Easter into many homes.

---

11 Easter
Easter Crosses

OBJECTIVE: To teach children the significance of the empty cross

Appropriate for ages 5 to 12

"'Don't be alarmed,' he said. 'You are looking for Jesus the Nazarene, Who was crucified. He has risen! He is not here.'"
— Mark 16:6 (NIV)

As you share with your pupils the wonderful story of Easter and the empty cross, let them make a cross, one of the significant Easter symbols to hang up at home.

This empty cross can be made with light-weight wire and colored tissue paper. Shape the wire into a cross. Spread a thin layer of rubber cement on a piece of tissue paper. Place the wire cross on the tissue paper. Use the other piece of tissue paper to cover the other side of the cross. When the cement has dried, trim the excess paper from the edges of the cross. Punch a hole at the top of the cross, and use thread or yarn to hang it.

With younger children, supervise the use of the wire carefully. Tape the two wire ends together with duct tape, then give to the child to bend into a cross shape.

Completed Cross

12 Easter
New Life

OBJECTIVE: To help children understand that the resurrection of Christ means Christ came alive again

Appropriate for ages 6 to 12

*"It is sown a natural body;
it is raised a spiritual body."*
— I Corinthians 15:44

This is an Easter custom from West Africa that will help teach your pupils about Christ's resurrection. Families are encouraged to plant seeds on Good Friday as they think of the sacrifice of Christ. Then they await the resurrection of the plants as they think about the resurrection of Christ.

Purchase several kinds of seeds and rewrap them in plastic sandwich bags or squares of plastic wrap. Attach to each seed bag a slip of paper with one of the following Scripture references written on it: I Corinthians 15:20-22, 35-38, 42-44, 50, 53-58. Include a note about the West African custom. Suggest that each person read the various Scriptures while they wait to see what "body" God has chosen to give their seeds. The seed bags can be stapled to the church bulletin on Palm Sunday or handed out during Sunday school. No one will know what kind of seeds they have received until they begin growing.

13 Easter
Easter Lilies

OBJECTIVE: To teach children the significance of Jesus' resurrection

Appropriate for ages 3 to 9

"He is not here, but is risen."
— Luke 24:6

Fill a paper cup with plaster of Paris. Set a 10-inch dowel rod (¼ inch in diameter) in the center of the cup as the plaster hardens. After the plaster of Paris is dry, let children cover the dowel by carefully wrapping it with strips of green crepe paper or florist's tape. Add a construction paper leaf or two. Wrap the cup with foil. A yellow bow can be added.

To make lilies, have children trace their hand on white construction paper. (Trace loosely.) Cut out each hand and curl the fingers backwards with a pencil. Then glue the little finger to the thumb to create a lily. A small piece of yellow construction paper can be shredded as shown in the illustration and then glued into the center of the lily. Attach the lily to the dowel stem with more crepe paper or florist's tape.

The lily tree makes a wonderful centerpiece for an Easter learning center. The children can make two lilies so they have one to take home.

14 Easter
An Easter Acrostic

OBJECTIVE: To help children learn that Easter is all about Jesus coming alive

Appropriate for ages 8 to 12

"The Son of Man must be delivered into the hands of sinful men, and be crucified, and the third day rise again."
— Luke 24:7

Read the Easter story from Luke 23 and 24. Have the children try to guess the word that goes with each letter of the word EASTER. Write the puzzle on the chalkboard for all to see or duplicate it for each child.

Answers: emptiness, angel, sepulchre, tomb, Easter, Redeemer.

E is for the ___ ___ ___ ___ ___ ___ ___ ___ ___ of the tomb on that morn.

A is for the ___ ___ ___ ___ ___ who rolled back the stone.

S for the ___ ___ ___ ___ ___ ___ ___ ___ ___ in Joseph's beautiful garden.

T for the ___ ___ ___ ___ that could not contain our Lord.

E is for ___ ___ ___ ___ ___ ___, the day of Christ's triumph.

R for the ___ ___ ___ ___ ___ ___ ___ ___ Who saves us from sin.

Pentecost — Seventh Sunday after Easter

The Festival of Pentecost is rich in images which portray the excitement of the coming of the Holy Spirit. The Apostles were in the Upper Room when a sound like a rushing mighty wind filled the house. There appeared to be tongues of fire falling upon them filling them with power to be witnesses for Christ.

What a wonderful time to give praise and thanksgiving for the way God prepares for this celebration of the birth of the Christian church.

15 Pentecost
Praise Festival

OBJECTIVE: To encourage the children to grasp the excitement of the Holy Spirit's presence

Appropriate for ages 3 to 12

"But ye shall receive power, after that the Holy Ghost is come upon you: and ye shall be witnesses unto me both in Jerusalem, and in all Judaea, and in Samaria, and unto the uttermost part of the earth."
— Acts 1:8

Have a grand surprise party for the whole family of God. The following are some suggestions for the celebration.

Plan a parade. Have balloons filled with air to symbolize the mighty rushing wind. Make banners of burlap and felt with words and symbols attached such as flames, a bunch of grapes (fruits of the Spirit), sheaths of wheat (harvest), and the words JOY, PEACE, and HALLELUJAH. The children can carry their banners and balloons as they march around the church or outside the church, singing songs of praise.

Call people to ministry. Make signs to place on the door of each classroom saying, "You are now entering your Field of Ministry." Symbolize the Spirit's calling of each one to minister by pinning a length of red yarn or ribbon on his or her shoulder.

The Holy Spirit gives gifts to each of God's

children. Our children can prepare gifts for others to symbolize this act. Encourage the boys and girls to make a gift at home during the week and to keep it a surprise until the end of the Pentecost celebration. Then...surprise! They give their gifts to people in the congregation: shut-ins, grandparents, and others.

Children's Day — May 5

To Jesus, children were considered a gift from God. Jesus clearly expressed His love and respect for children and commanded His disciples to do the same.

Children need to know they are special and wonderful because they are made in the image of God. Many problems can be averted both now and in later years if children have a good self-image . . . if they can see themselves as Jesus sees them.

16 Children's Day
This Is What I Can Do

OBJECTIVE: To foster positive self-esteem in each child

Appropriate for ages 3 to 12

"Now therefore hearken unto me, O ye children: for blessed are they that keep my ways."
— Proverbs 8:32

Discuss with the children the things the world looks at such as fancy clothes, lots of money and possessions, fancy houses and cars, jewelry, lots of "things." Trying to achieve these things often leads children to do wrong in order to get the money or item needed. It can cause arguments with parents and friends, and can lead to feelings of despair when the child is put down by peers. We want to help children see themselves as God sees them. He looks at the things that are important such as our attitudes, what we do with the talents and abilities He gave us, how we treat others, and how we treat Him.

The week before Children's Day explain to the boys and girls that on their special day, you are going to invite parents, friends, and the entire congregation to see the things the children can do. They are to bring samples of their hobbies to class the following week, and samples of their creative

expression in the form of songs, poems, art, work, etc. Help them compose a class litany or song about their being made in the image of God that can be presented for the guests. The students can also help prepare refreshments to serve to the guests.

National Day of Prayer — First Thursday in May

Repeatedly, Jesus stressed the importance of prayer — in His teachings as well in His own life. He often retreated away from the crowds to spend time in prayer. Even His final days on earth were marked with frequent and intense prayers to His Father.

The task facing children's leaders is to encourage boys and girls to want to communicate with God in prayer. Learning to pray is a life-long journey, and the natural faith of a child gives him or her a head start. If we can help children develop sound attitudes and teach them basic truths about God and prayer, we can guide them in growing into mature Christians.

17 National Day of Prayer
Follow-the-Leader Prayer

OBJECTIVE: To help each child learn to communicate with God in prayer

Appropriate for ages 3 to 12

"Hearken unto the voice of my cry, my King, and my God: for unto Thee will I pray."
— Psalm 5:2

To help children become more confident in praying aloud, introduce the follow-the-leader prayer. Each child will have the opportunity to say one or two sentences or to pray silently and then give the next child a chance to do the same. The last student or the teacher may end the prayer.

At prayer time, gather the children into a circle. Before beginning, select two children who are usually willing to pray aloud or ask for volunteers to open and close the prayer time. With younger children, it is best for the teacher to begin and end the prayer time. Explain that after the first person prays aloud, the person to her left should follow with a short prayer, either aloud or silent. Each person, whether praying silently or aloud, should end his prayer by saying, "Amen." This lets the next person know that it is her turn.

Having a theme for your prayer time, such as

things to thank God for or friends and family, can be helpful in stimulating participation. Be careful not to push anyone who is not ready to pray aloud.

Mother's Day — Second Sunday in May

Since the days of antiquity, people have expressed their love and respect for their mothers. In medieval England, young people who worked as servants and apprentices were permitted to go home once a year on a Sunday to visit their mothers. This was called Mothering Sunday, and the children took flowers and sweet cakes home.

Mother's Day started officially in 1914 in the United States. A red carnation is worn to honor living mothers and a white carnation is worn in remembrance of mothers who are no longer living.

18 Mother's Day
Bible Mothers Quiz

OBJECTIVE: To challenge children to show their love and respect for their mothers every day

Appropriate for ages 3 to 12

"Children, obey your parents in the Lord: for this is right."
— Ephesians 6:1

Duplicate the quiz below for each child. The children can use their Bibles to help find the answers. See how many mothers you can name.

As these mothers and their children discovered, it is important for children to show their love and respect for their mothers.

Answers: *1. Elisheba (Moses' mother), 2. Mary (Jesus' mother), 3. Hannah, 4. Rebekah, 5. Eve, 6. Elisabeth (Elizabeth), 7. Rachel, 8. Sarah*

Name the Mother Quiz

1. What mother hid her baby in a tiny basket boat? (Exodus 6:20)

2. What mother went to a wedding feast and asked her son to help? (John 2:1)

3. What mother prayed for a baby boy and when he was older took him to live and work in the Tabernacle? (I Samuel 1:20)

4. What mother had twin sons? (Genesis 24:51)

5. Who was the first mother? (Genesis 3:20)

6. What mother had a son who preached in the wilderness? (Luke 1:13)

7. What mother had a son whom his brothers sold to be a slave in Egypt? (Genesis 29:20)

8. What mother laughed when she heard she would have a child? (Genesis 21:1)

19 Mother's Day
Mother's Day Coupon Book

OBJECTIVE: To challenge children to be helpers to their mothers every day

Appropriate for ages 3 to 12

"A woman who fears the LORD is to be praised."
— Proverbs 31:30 (NIV)

Help children make a Book of Promises for Mother. Make a cover by cutting a sheet of colored construction paper in half, width-wise. Fold one of the halves in half and print "For Mother" on the top page. Provide several sheets of plain paper for the book pages.

The boys and girls can write on each page of their Coupon Book a promise to do something for Mother. Young children may choose a pre-made page to color. Mother can tear out and redeem the coupons as things need to be done. Some suggestions might be: one cheerful dish washing, one thorough room cleaning, running one errand.

20 Mother's Day
Giant Mother's Day Card

OBJECTIVE: To challenge children to show their love for their mothers in a special way

Appropriate for ages 3 to 12

*"'Honor your father and mother'—
which is the first commandment with a promise—
'that it may go well with you and that you may
enjoy long life on the earth.'"*
— Ephesians 6:2-3 (NIV)

Help younger children make the "World's Biggest Mother's Day Card Ever" to show their love for their mothers in a big way. Older children will need minimal assistance. Provide a 42-inch long sheet of poster paper and a 12-inch length of ribbon for each child. Have each child stretch out full-length on a strip of the butcher paper while you outline his silhouette with a crayon.

Print "Happy Mother's Day from (child's name)," and "Thank You, God, for my mother" around the outline. The children can sign the card and color or paint it to match the color of her hair, eyes, and clothing. Roll up each card and tie it with the ribbon.

Memorial Day — Last Monday in May

Memorial Day is a special day to honor and remember the men and women who gave their lives defending the United States and other friendly countries.

This day is also called Decoration Day because people place flowers of remembrance on the graves of their loved ones.

21 Memorial Day
Giving All in Love

OBJECTIVE: To challenge children to make right choices and to help others

Appropriate for ages 3 to 12

"Greater love hath no man than this, that a man lay down his life for his friends."
— John 15:13

Perhaps the most significant way to honor our fallen soldiers is to teach peaceful ways to settle arguments. Talk with the children about ways to be heroic other than in fighting wars. They can speak up for what is right, not go along with their peers when wrong actions are suggested, make friends with new children in their school or neighborhood, settle arguments peacefully, and cooperate with others. A real hero is someone who makes contributions to all people in medicine, law, government, the arts, education, etc.

Let the children think of ways they can be heroes now by helping others or by choosing right over wrong. Then prepare hero medals for each child to wear as a reminder. Cut circles from construction paper and mount them on lightweight cardboard or frozen orange juice can lids.

Decorate the medals with gold stars, ribbons, and colorful designs. Tape or glue a safety pin to the back. Pin the medal to the child's shirt.

Flag Day — June 14

Flag day is a day of national observance of the birthday of the flag of the United States of America. The Continental Congress in 1777 adopted this banner as our national flag. The red represents the hardiness and courage of our nation; blue symbolizes justice, vigilance, and perseverance; and white emphasizes the purity and innocence of new found liberty.

The Christian church also has a flag that symbolizes the kingdom of God on earth. Flag Day is an appropriate time to teach children about the Christian flag and its meaning as well as the flag of their country.

22 Flag Day
Happy Birthday, Old Glory

OBJECTIVE: That children will learn respect for the flag of the United States and the Christian flag

Appropriate for ages 3 to 12

*"In the Name of our God
we will set up our banners."*
— Psalm 20:5

Our flag, Old Glory, is the proudest symbol of our nation. We love our nation and are proud of it. We fly our flag at all government offices, schools, churches, and many homes and businesses. When the flag passes by in a parade, people stand to their feet, men remove their hats, people place their hands over their hearts, and servicemen and women raise their hands in salute and stand at attention. The flag is never to be dragged on the ground and cannot be used as a tablecloth or clothing — it must be shown respect at all times.

The Christian flag stands for the kingdom of God on earth. It has a pledge of allegiance, just as our national flag. The pledge to the Christian flag goes like this:

"I pledge allegiance to the Christian flag, and to the Saviour for whose kingdom it stands; one brotherhood, uniting Christians everywhere in service and in love."

Display both flags in the classroom and lead

the children in saying both pledges. Provide red, white, and blue construction paper so the children can make each flag to take home for their rooms. They can cut the stars and stripes and cross out of the appropriate colors and glue them to the background (or provide star stickers).

Father's Day — Third Sunday in June

Father's Day was started in 1924 to honor fathers. A red rose is worn to honor living fathers, and a white rose is worn to remember fathers who are no longer living.

Jesus clearly expressed God's command to obey parents. Father's Day provides an opportunity for children to learn the importance of honoring and obeying their fathers.

23 Father's Day
Bible Fathers Quiz

OBJECTIVE: To encourage children to honor their fathers and to give them a few ways to do so

Appropriate for ages 3 to 12

"Children, obey your parents in the Lord: for this is right. Honour thy father and mother."
— Ephesians 6:1-2

Children can use their Bible to help them find the answers to the quiz questions. The quiz may be completed individually or as a class. Younger children may be told the Bible stories first, followed by the questions. Be prepared to help them with the answers.

After the children complete the quiz, discuss ways of honoring parents (helping, sharing, making the bed, setting the table, etc.).

Answers: 1. *Solomon*, 2. *Zebedee*, 3. *Abraham*, 4. *Jairus*, 5. *Isaac*, 6. *Zecharias (Zechariah)*, 7. *Noah*, 8. *David*

Who Was the Father Quiz

1. What father built the great Temple in Jerusalem? (I Kings 8:22)

2. What father had two fishermen sons who became Jesus' followers? (Matthew 4:21)

3. What man was called the father of his people? (Genesis 18:18)

4. What father came to Jesus that He might heal his sick daughter? (Luke 8:41)

5. What father had twin sons and was deceived by one of them? (Genesis 27:22)

6. What father became speechless until his son was born? (Luke 1:13)

7. What father was the first sailor? (Genesis 6:9)

8. What father went from sling to throne? (II Samuel 5:25)

24 Father's Day
Father's Day Card

OBJECTIVE: To help children bring joy to their fathers and to give them some ways to do this

Appropriate for ages 3 to 12

"A wise son brings joy to his father."
— Proverbs 10:1 (NIV)

Have each child make a Father's Day card. Help them fold a 9 x 13-inch piece of paper in half. Draw a shirt collar and necktie on the front. Let the children color designs on the tie and shirt. Provide buttons for them to glue to the shirt front.

Print "Dear Dad" on the front. On the inside of the card print, "I'm tie-ing my love in this gift for you. Check off each project as I complete it." Below this have the children list several service projects they can help Dad with such as mowing the lawn and taking out the trash. At least five items should be listed with a box by each item that Dad can check when the project is finished.

25 Father's Day
Dad's Car Bag

OBJECTIVE: To help children honor their fathers with a special gift

Appropriate for ages 3 to 12

"Honour thy father and mother."
— Ephesians 6:2

Dad's Car Bag is an easy gift to make for father on his day. Provide each child with a plastic bag (similar in size to those used for car litter bags). Cut a hole near the top of one side (the back side) of the bag so it can be hung over a knob or door handle in a car.

Let the children use felt tip pens to decorate the fronts of the bags. You might suggest that they draw pictures of something their fathers like to do such as fishing, gardening, golfing, etc. Have them print "My Dad" or "Dad's Trash" or a clever saying on the bag.

Independence Day — July 4th

Independence Day reminds us of the signing of the Declaration of Independence on July 4, 1776. This date marks the birthday of the United States of America. When we think of America, we think of a land of freedom. But America will only be free as long as her people look to Christ for leadership and guidance. We celebrate that freedom on the Fourth of July.

Ask your pupils to promise God that they will always look into His Word to find guidance for their lives so that they will be free in Christ. Pray for God's help as they make this promise.

26 Independence Day
God and Country

OBJECTIVE: To inspire and nurture a spirit of love and loyalty to God and country

Appropriate for ages 4 to 12

"If the Son sets you free, you will be free indeed."
— John 8:36 (NIV)

Children associate July 4th with fireworks, so let them make a rocket. Explain that like the rocket which contains explosive powder, we can be filled with the Holy Spirit and receive much more power than fireworks have. Also, fireworks explode and their power is gone as the sparks die falling to the ground. The power we receive from Jesus through the Holy Spirit will not die. The Holy Spirit will see us through all that life has to offer and then will get us to Heaven.

Provide a cardboard tube (paper towel roll) and red, white, and blue construction paper for each child to use. Let the children cut a piece of construction paper to glue around the tube, covering it completely. Next, have them cut a circle a little larger than the opening of the tube. Help them cut a slit to the center of the circle and bend it around to make a cone. Glue it together; then glue the cone to the end of the tube. Decorate the rocket with gold stars or with markers or crayons. Print on the rocket, "Filled with the power of God."

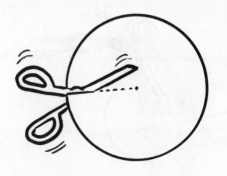
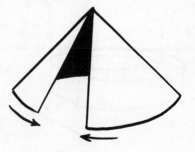
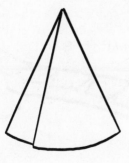

Promotion Day — August or September

Graduation day in the Sunday school is a time when children have an opportunity to display their achievements from the past year in Bible study, memory work, attendance, and to be recognized for the completion of special assignments or outstanding accomplishments.

Consider presenting special certificates to the students to recognize their efforts. Arrange displays in the room which show the projects the boys and girls have completed during the year. Invite parents and friends to visit the room with their child. Encourage the children to be tour guides, explaining the various projects and displays.

27 Promotion Day
Graduation

OBJECTIVE: To encourage children to study the Word of God so they can grow in stature and wisdom

Appropriate for ages 3 to 12

*"Desire the . . . milk of the Word,
that ye may grow thereby."*
— I Peter 2:2

Make simple crowns for the younger children to wear. Graduation caps would also be appropriate for all ages. To make each cap, cut a 10-inch poster board square and a 3 x 20-inch construction paper strip. Fold down one inch along the long edge of the strip and cut notches in the folded part. Staple the strip into a circle and glue the notched edge to the poster board square.

For each tassel cut eleven 10-inch pieces of crochet yarn. Tie ten pieces of yarn at their center with the other 10-inch piece of yarn. Fold the pieces of yarn in half and tie securely with a piece of thread or string a half inch below the center fold. Tape the tassel inside the cap.

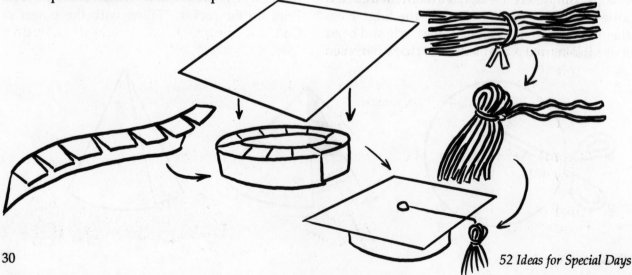

Labor Day — First Monday in September

Labor Day was started in 1882 as a holiday to honor both the workers and their work. Conduct an informal discussion with your children about starting back to school (which to them means work), and the work they hope to do when they are grown. Also discuss the kind of study and training they will need for that occupation.

Have the children read the following Scripture references: Ecclesiastes 9:10a, I Corinthians 3:9a, and II Thessalonians 3:10c. Explain that God wants us to labor with Him. He is not pleased with laziness.

28 Labor Day
A Mind to Work

OBJECTIVE: To help children learn the necessity and blessing of work; to assure them of God's help

Appropriate for ages 9 to 12

"This we commanded you, that if any would not work, neither should he eat."
— II Thessalonians 3:10

Bring pictures or actual replicas of tools and other implements used by workers in the Bible. As you hold up each item for the children to see, ask them to guess who in the Bible used the item and what their occupation might have been. If no one can guess, give the Scripture reference and let the children see who can find the answer first.

1. (Shepherd's crook) The shepherds
   — Luke 2:8.

2. (Saw or hammer) Joseph the carpenter
   — Matthew 13:55.

3. (Fishing nets) Peter, Andrew, James and John — Matthew 4:18-21.

4. (Coins or abacus) Matthew the tax collector
   — Matthew 9:9.

5. (Bag of coins) Zacchaeus, a rich man
   — Luke 19:2.

6. (Sword) A Centurion from Capernaum (army officer) — Luke 7:8.

7. (Small tent) Paul the tentmaker
   — Acts 18:1, 3.

8. (Rich purple cloth) Lydia the cloth seller
   — Acts 16:14.

9. (Needle and thread) Dorcas the seamstress
   — Acts 9:39.

10. (Medicine) Luke the doctor
    — Colossians 4:14.

11. (Scroll or Bible) Timothy the preacher
    — I Tim. 4:13; II Tim 2:15.

Back to School — September

Summer is over and we are all being drawn back from vacations to begin a new year of school, both secular and Christian. The family of God represented in the Sunday school has been separated by so many being away during the summer.

September is a time to welcome everyone "home" and to provide encouragement and enthusiasm for the exciting possibilities that lie ahead.

29 Back to School
Homecoming

OBJECTIVE: To nurture a sense of family among the children in the household of God

Appropriate for ages 3 to 12

"For ye are all the children of God by faith in Christ Jesus."
— Galatians 3:26

Send invitations to everyone in the Sunday school and to those who once were members but have perhaps moved away or have been gone for some other reason. Prepare special posters and bulletin boards in every classroom to welcome everyone back.

Plan an all-Sunday school picnic or pot-luck dinner with lots of music, games and contests to follow for all age groups. Make a collage of activities from the past year announcing the Sunday School Homecoming. Take pictures of each class during the homecoming event and, when developed, hang them in the church foyer to build excitement for the coming year.

Grandparent's Day — Second Sunday in September

The Bible is filled with examples of older believers working with younger ones to encourage and guide them. Paul thanked God for Timothy's faith which lived in his grandmother, his mother and also in him.

Children need to know that grandparents deserve their respect and honor, and that they are valuable members of God's household of faith. They also need to be guided by the living example of older Christians.

30 Grandparent's Day
Grandparents Join the Class

OBJECTIVE: To encourage children to show their appreciation for older Christian adults

Appropriate for ages 3 to 9

"My son, pay attention to my wisdom, listen well to my words of insight."
— Proverbs 5:1 (NIV)

Many children do not live near their grandparents, and as a result, only see them once or twice a year. Providing children with opportunities to interact with older adults helps them begin to appreciate the wisdom and experience that only an older generation can offer.

Have boys and girls send invitations to their grandparents to visit their class on Grandparents Day. Children who do not have grandparents living nearby may adopt an older person in the congregation for the day. Urge the "grandparents" to participate in every activity in the class along with the children.

The week before the grandparents' visit, have the children write special "love" messages to each visitor. Help the children hide the love messages around the classroom before their grandparents arrive on their special day. As part of the festivi-

ties, the guests must search the room (with the help of the children) to find their messages. Encourage each child to serve the grandparents at snack time, offer them a chair, and act as their host throughout the class session.

Columbus Day — October 12

In October we remember Columbus' voyage to the New World with his three ships, the Niña, the Pinta, and the Santa Maria. Christopher Columbus had difficulty receiving permission and getting the money and help he needed to make his journey. Many times we experience difficulty when there are things we must do.

Children need to be encouraged that when God asks us to do something, He will help us along the way. He will provide the means, clear the way, and give the strength we need to accomplish the task.

31 Columbus Day
Overcoming Difficulties

OBJECTIVE: To help children have faith to go forward in the strength of the Lord

Appropriate for ages 3 to 9

"Notwithstanding the Lord stood with me, and strengthened me."
— II Timothy 4:17

Let the children make commemorative pictures of one of Columbus' ships to remind them of God's strength. Duplicate the ship pattern from page 35 for each child. Let each child cut out a ship and glue it on a sheet of blue construction paper. They can color the ship, draw waves in the water and a sun or clouds in the sky. Provide drinking straw halves and fabric to create sails and cotton balls for clouds. At the top of the picture have each child print the words, "Go in the strength of the Lord."

If time allows, bring shaving cream for the children to make whitecaps or waves on their blue ocean. Squirt a small amount of shaving cream on each paper and let the children use their fingers to form the cream into waves. Provide

small-size men's shirts for smocks and bring wet paper towels for clean-up.

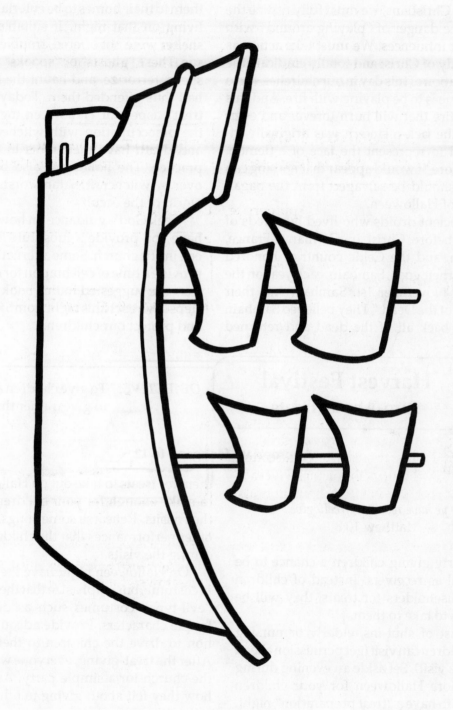

Harvest Festival (Halloween Alternatives)
— October 31

As Christians, we must fully realize the extreme danger of "playing around" with satanic influences. We must take action as the body of Christ and totally eradicate the celebration of this day in our churches, for to continue is to be playing with fire. And this is the fire that will burn forever and ever. Even the jack-o-lantern was originally intended to represent the face of a demon. Therefore, it would appear that nothing can be or should be salvaged from the pagan event of Halloween.

Ancient druids who lived hundreds of years before Christ in Germany, France, Britain, and the Celtic countries honored one of their gods, Samhain, each year on the eve of November 1st. Samhain was their "Lord of the Dead." They believed Samhain called back all of the dead and returned them to their homes to be entertained by the living on that night. If suitable food and shelter were not offered, trouble would ensue, These "ghosts" or "spooks" would cast spells, terrorize, and haunt the living who had thus offended them. Today's "trick or treat" aspect of Halloween together with the preoccupation with witches, demons, and death have their roots in this pagan practice. The holiday is also being taken over by witchcraft, Satan worship, and the world of the occult.

Seek God's guidance on how He would have you provide a substitute for Halloween in His church. Some alternative ways to provide a time of celebration for our youngsters are suggested in this book as we take steps to wrench this night from Satan's grasp and protect our children.

32 Harvest Festival
Turn-About Treats

OBJECTIVE: To give children an opportunity to give, rather than receive

Appropriate for ages 5 to 12

"Freely ye have received, freely give."
— Matthew 10:8

Plan a party giving children a chance to be givers as well as receivers. Instead of children besieging householders for treats, they will be making treats to take to them.

Make a list of shut-ins, elderly or nursing homes the children can visit (get permission ahead of time for the visit). Set aside an evening during the week before Halloween for your children (and parents) to have a "treat preparation" night. Make cookies, popcorn balls, and candy and wrap them for treats to take out on Halloween. Be sure to make enough for your children to enjoy after their visits. Rehearse some songs, recitations, or other performances that the children can present during the visits.

On Halloween night have the children dress in costume, but emphasize that there should be no "evil-type" costumes such as demons or grotesque characters. Provide adequate transportation to drive the children to their destinations. After the treat-giving, everyone will meet back at the church for a simple party. Ask the children how they felt about giving to others rather than just getting.

33 **Harvest Festival**
Paper Bag Costume Party

OBJECTIVE: To help children stay away from evil influences

Appropriate for ages 5 to 12

*"Be not overcome of evil,
but overcome evil with good."*
— Romans 12:21

Instead of letting children spend lots of money for costumes to wear to your Sunday school party, tell them they will make a mask as a party activity. Provide a large paper bag (grocery bag) for each child. Have available construction paper, crepe paper, cotton balls, straw, yarn, foil, crayons, markers, glue, scissors, and anything else you can imagine that could be used to decorate the bags.

As children arrive, give them a bag and let them design their own mask. Be sure they understand that demons or grotesque masks are not allowed. Explain that we want to avoid the evil these represent. Help younger children with drawing eye holes and cutting them out. Give prizes for the funniest, prettiest, saddest, ugliest, etc., masks (award prizes by age groups so small children are not competing against older children).

Another twist to this idea is to plan a party in which everyone who attends must be dressed like a clown. Encourage the children to invite their friends. Give prizes for the clowns who are the ugliest, funniest, prettiest, saddest, etc. Decorate the room with balloons, streamers, pictures of clowns, clown masks, and circus animals. Have a "three-ring circus" by designating separate areas

for activities such as refreshments, games, and circus tricks (every clown must perform by singing, dancing, playing an instrument, giving a reading, etc.).

Provide refreshments of animal crackers or cupcakes with an animal cracker standing on top. Place sherbet in the punch to give it a frothy appearance.

Conclude with a Bible story and a discussion of ways the children can "do good" at home, at school, and at church. Everyone will have a fun and safe time.

Thanksgiving — Fourth Thursday in November

Pilgrims came to America from England in 1620 seeking religious freedom. Their first winter was very hard but they survived and learned how to farm. Their second harvest was bountiful and by decree of Governor William Bradford, the Pilgrims held a festival of Thanksgiving in 1621.

Eighty friendly Indians came to help the pilgrims. Their feasting, praying, singing, and playing lasted for three days. Today, at Thanksgiving time, we give thanks for the fullness of our lives and the blessings we receive from God.

34 Thanksgiving
Pilgrims and Indians

OBJECTIVE: To encourage children to be thankful for their Christian heritage of Thanksgiving

Appropriate for ages 3 to 9

"It is a good thing to give thanks unto the Lord."
— Psalm 92:1

Tell the story of Thanksgiving and how the Indians, our native Americans, helped the Pilgrims when they came to America looking for freedom to worship God as they wished. Provide a large paper bag for each child. You will also need construction paper, scissors and glue.

Duplicate pattern pages 39 and 40 for each child. Let the children cut out the patterns from construction paper and color them to make a Pilgrim and Indian. Help them follow the directions on the patterns. Precut the figures for younger children. Show them how to form the Pilgrim on one side of the paper bag and the Indian on the opposite side. On one side of the bag, print the scripture reference.

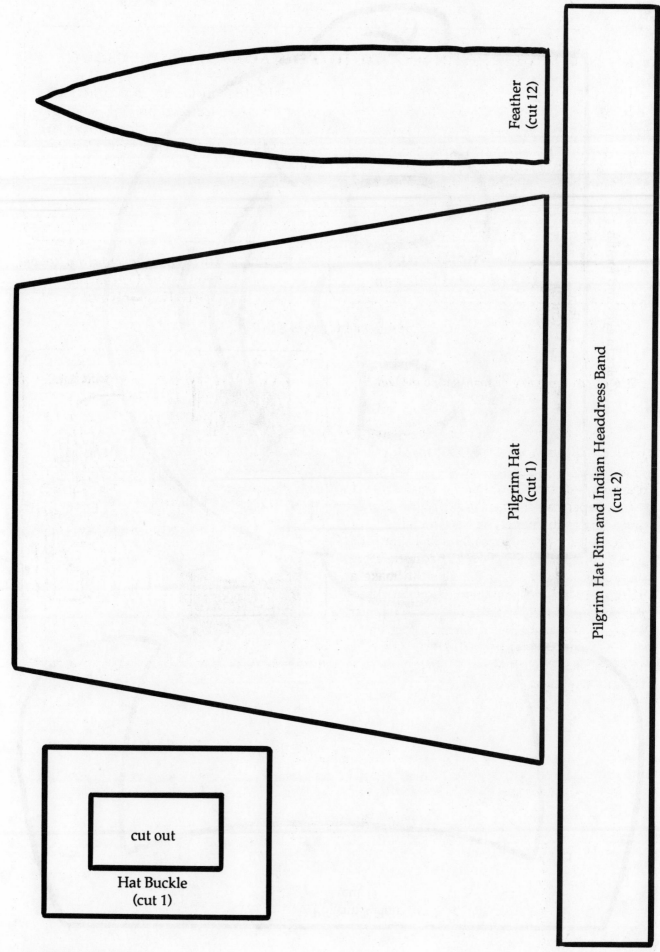

Feather
(cut 12)

Pilgrim Hat
(cut 1)

Pilgrim Hat Rim and Indian Headdress Band
(cut 2)

cut out

Hat Buckle
(cut 1)

Color in eyes and mouth

Face
(cut 2)

Pilgrim's Hair
(cut 1)

40

35 Thanksgiving
Thanksgiving Notes

OBJECTIVE: To help children understand that you are thankful for them

Appropriate for ages 3 to 9

*"O give thanks unto the Lord; for He is good:
for His mercy endureth for ever."*
— Psalm 136:1

Send a Thanksgiving note to each of your students. Duplicate the pattern below or design one of your own. Make it personal. Thank each child for something special he contributes to the group — his cheerful smile, the way she has helped in class, something he brought to share, her friendliness to visitors, his good work each week, etc.

Along with the note enclose a copy of the giant turkey from page 42 for the children to color and bring to Sunday school on Thanksgiving Sunday. This will not only encourage attendance, but will help the children have the positive reinforcement necessary for good self-esteem.

Give thanks unto the Lord.
—— Psalm 136:1

Happy
Thanksgiving!

Thank you . . .

Color the turkey and bring it to Sunday school next week.

Thanksgiving
Thanksgiving Fun

OBJECTIVE: To teach children that God's blessings bring happiness

Appropriate for ages 5 to 12

"My soul shall be joyful in the Lord."
— Psalm 35:9

Turkey Shoot. Blow up small paper bags and close them with rubber bands. Hide these "turkeys" all over the room or yard. Send the children out to hunt for the turkeys. When a child finds one, he may pop it. The child bringing in the most popped bags is the greatest hunter.

Turkey Dodge. The children form a circle with one child in the center. Those around the circle are the Pilgrims and Indians. The child in the center is the turkey. To start, one child in the circle throws a foam ball (or other lightweight ball) and tries to hit the turkey. No fair hitting above the waist! The turkey tries to get away from the ball. The child nearest the ball after it misses, picks it up and throws it at the turkey. When a child hits the turkey, he and the turkey change places. Try to let every child throw the ball or be the turkey.

Turkey Treat. Give each child a round chocolate sandwich cookie, a malted milk ball, several candy corn pieces, a small cinnamon candy, a plastic knife, and a small amount of chocolate frosting. Help each child open the cookie and dab a small amount of frosting in the center of one cookie half. Place the malted milk ball on the frosting. Dab frosting near the top of the milk ball

and place a cinnamon candy on it.

Spread frosting in the center of the remaining cookie half and make an arc of frosting above the center. Place five or six candy corns in the arc as turkey feathers. Attach the cookie to the back of the milk ball, so the feathers frame the milk ball, to complete the turkey. Provide additional cookies and candy for snacking. If time allows, let the children make two turkeys so they can eat one and take one home. Talk about God's blessings as the children work.

Advent — The four weeks before Christmas

Advent is a time when we can draw closer together in our anticipation of God's gift to the world — His Son. It is a time to prepare our hearts and minds for Christmas and to change our attitudes from "getting" to "giving." It is through giving that we are drawn closer to both God and our fellow brothers and sisters in Christ.

37   Advent
Family Advent Wreath

OBJECTIVE: To draw the family together to prepare spiritually for the birth of Jesus

Appropriate for ages 3 to 12

"Behold, a virgin shall be with child, and shall bring forth a Son, and they shall call His name Emmanuel, which being interpreted is, God with us."
— Matthew 1:23

What a wonderful time of year to help families develop the important habit of having family devotions. Plan an evening in late November, before the beginning of Advent, when families can come together for a time of fellowship. During this evening, each family will work together to make their own Advent wreath to use at home during the coming weeks until Christmas.

You will need the following materials for each family. A heavy cardboard circle at least twelve to fourteen inches in diameter. Do not cut out the center of the cardboard, for you will need this to hold candles. Make small holes in the cardboard in order to slip thin wire through to tie on the boughs. Provide several boughs of greens (cedar, pine, etc.) for each family. They can trim these as desired and wire them to their cardboard base.

Each family will need five candles (one of which should be white), some narrow red ribbon, and some 1-inch wide white ribbon. Tacky glue or self-hardening clay can be used to hold the candles in place on the wreath. The white candle should be placed in the center with the other four making a circle around it. Cut the red ribbon into 2-inch pieces. Fold each piece over at the center to make a loop. Glue these red loops among the boughs to represent berries. Make a large bow with the white ribbon and attach it to the wreath. Duplicate the guide below for each family to use with their Advent wreath devotions.

Advent Wreath Devotions

The circle, with no beginning and no end, stands for the eternity of God. The evergreens represent life and growth.

Five candles represent the four Sundays of Advent and the day of Jesus' birth.

Red represents the blood Jesus shed for us. White represents the purity of Jesus.

Week 1.   Light the first candle: Prophecy Candle. Read Isaiah 7:14 and Isaiah 9:2-6. Sing "Oh, Come, Oh, Come, Emmanuel" and "It Came Upon the Midnight Clear."

Week 2.   Light the first and second candles: Bethlehem Candle. Read Micah 5:2-4. Sing "O Little Town of Bethlehem" and "The First Noel."

Week 3.   Light first, second, and third candles: Shepherd's Candle. Read Luke 2:8-20. Sing "Go Tell It on the Mountain."

Week 4.   Light first, second, third, and fourth candles: Star and Angel Candle. Read Matthew 2:1-12. Sing "Hark! The Herald Angels Sing."

Christmas Eve. Light the first four plus the center white candle: Christ Candle. Read Luke 2:1-20. Sing "Joy to The World" and "Oh, Come All Ye Faithful."

38 Advent
Advent Giving Tree

OBJECTIVE: To help children understand the importance of giving and sharing the spirit of Christmas

Appropriate for ages 6 to 12

"It is more blessed to give than to receive."
— Acts 20:35

Help your children share the spirit of Christmas by providing an Advent Giving Tree for each one. Duplicate the tree on page 46 onto green construction paper for each child. Duplicate this page onto white construction paper. The ornaments on the Advent tree are numbered, and each one has something the child is to do on that day, starting with December 1st.

Provide tape, scissors, colored glue, puff paints, markers, crayons, and construction paper of various colors. Have the children cut twenty-four ¾-inch circles and decorate them with various colors and designs to cover the ornaments on the tree. Tape the top of each circle to the tree so that when the circle is lifted it reveals what is written underneath.

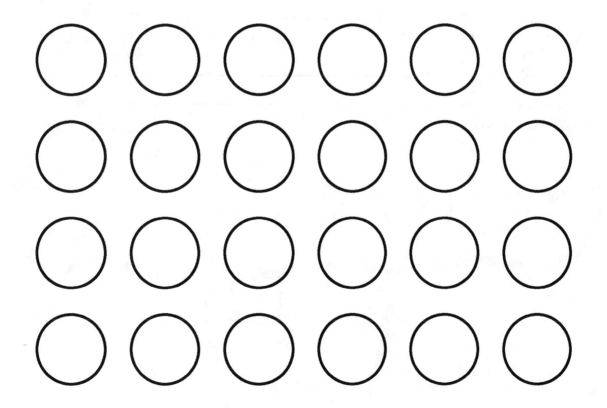

24 Give a gift to someone

23 Pray for a joyful Christmas

22 Help someone with a job

21 Share something with a friend

20 Sing a Christmas carol

19 Make a gift for someone

18 Clean up your room

16 Pray the Lord's Prayer

17 Keep a promise

15 Make up a Christmas poem

12 Make and send a Christmas card

13 Bake Christmas cookies

14 Do something for Mom or Dad

11 Make a Christmas decoration

6 Help set the table

7 Pray for someone you love

10 Do something nice for a teacher

9 Take out the trash

8 Make a Christmas picture

5 Do something nice for yourself

2 Write a letter to a grandparent

1 Make up a thank you prayer

3 Help do the dishes

4 Visit a friend

ADVENT TREE

39 Advent
Advent Bulletin Board

OBJECTIVE: To help children prepare their hearts and minds for Christmas

Appropriate for ages 3 to 12

"And she shall bring forth a Son, and thou shalt call His name JESUS: for He shall save His people from their sins."
— Matthew 1:21

Children may think of advent as a "countdown" to the days until Christmas. If so, help them realize the impact Christ's birth has in their lives. Create a giant Advent calendar for your room. An overall size of 4 x 7 feet would be ideal. You will need 24 pieces of either red or green 9 X 12-inch construction paper. Make an I shape in the center of each piece of paper (5 inches long in the center and 7 inches across the top and bottom). Cut along these lines to form doors which will be opened each of the days during Advent.

Across the top of each door print a date from December 1st through 24th. Locate some old Christmas cards and select 24 with religious themes. Glue or tape one of the cards behind each door. Attach the doors to your bulletin board to make a calendar. Across the top of the calendar

print, "PREPARING FOR CHRISTMAS."

Using the Advent calendar each Sunday, let the children open the doors for each day of the past week. Look at the pictures and talk about the Christmas story.

Hanukkah — December

Hannukah is an eight day Jewish Festival that occurs on the 25th day of the ninth month of the Jewish calendar. Hanukkah celebrates the cleansing of the Temple after its desecration by Antiochus. It is also called the Festival of Lights or the Feast of Dedication. Hanukkah was celebrated in Jesus' time and is still observed by Jews today.

In ancient times a tyrant named Antiochus wanted the Jews to give up their holy books and to worship idols instead of God. The Jewish Maccabees fought Antiochus and won. The Jews rejoiced and returned to their Temple to re-kindle the eternal light in the Temple lamp. But they could only find a very small jar of holy oil for the lamp. This small amount of oil would burn for only one night. They put the oil in the lamp (the Menorah, a candlestick with nine branches) anyway and a strange thing happened — it burned for eight days.

40 Hanukkah
Dreidel Game

OBJECTIVE: To help the children understand the customs and beliefs of others

Appropriate for ages 4 to 12

"And Jesus increased in wisdom and stature, and in favour with God and man."
— Luke 2:52

Jewish families celebrate this festival today by lighting the candles on their Menorah and by having parties with gifts, singing, celebrating, and lots of potato pancakes for everyone to eat. The children are given little spinning tops called dreidels, with the Hebrew letters NGHS, which signify, "A great miracle happened here."

Let the children play a dreidel game. Make a dreidel by securing one end of a toothpick in a cotton ball and stuffing the cotton ball tightly into a round-ended thimble. Tell the children about the festival of Hanukkah as they work. Explain that Jesus grew up in a Jewish home and that many Jews of Jesus' day celebrated Hanukkah.

Make a game board numbered like a clock face. The children take turns spinning the thimble-dreidel in the center of the board. Players write

down the numbers to which the stick points when it stops spinning. After a certain number of turns, or length of time, add up the numbers. Whoever has the greatest number of points is the winner.

Christmas — December 25

Christmas is the celebration of Jesus' birth. It is important for children to realize that everything about Jesus' birth was a special part of God's plan; it all happened for a reason. Although He was God's Son, Jesus was born in a lowly manger. This, too, was part of God's plan. Jesus' whole life and death happened for one important reason: to show people that He is the true Son of God, sent to earth to save us from our sins.

Some children may be confused about Jesus being God's Son rather than Joseph's. Help older children understand that God was Jesus' Father. Explain that the Baby Jesus in Bethlehem grew up to be the Christ of the cross. Remind the children that Jesus was a real person Who was born in Bethlehem and died on the cross and then came alive again for each of them.

41 Christmas
Christmas Wreath

OBJECTIVE: To help children remember the real reason for Christmas

Appropriate for ages 3 to 12

"For unto us a Child is born,
unto us a Son is given."
— Isaiah 9:6

At Christmas we see many doors with wreaths. Children can make one to hang in their room at home that will remind them of the reason for Christmas. A wreath is round and reminds us of God. God is Eternal (I Timothy 1:17), with no beginning nor ending. Provide a paper plate for each child. Cut out the center of the plate.

The candle reminds us that Christ is the Light of the World (John 3:19), so we too, are to let our lights shine (Matthew 5:16). Duplicate for each child the pattern for the candle from page 50. Help each child cut out a candle from yellow construction paper and glue the candle onto the paper plate so that it sticks up through the hole in the center of the wreath.

Green represents life and hope, and Jesus is the hope of the world (Joel 3:16b). Provide lots of green tissue paper cut into 3-inch squares. Let children crunch the tissue squares and glue them onto the wreath.

Red berries remind us that the Lord Jesus died on the cross, shed His blood, so that our sins would be forgiven. Either have small red pompons or red yarn to make berries. The children can glue several of these onto their wreath.

Help the children make a white bow out of ribbon or yarn that can be placed at the bottom of their wreath. This bow tells us that after we accept the Lord Jesus Christ as our Savior we are washed "white as snow" (Isaiah 1:18) and we receive Christ's Righteousness (Phil. 3:9).

Duplicate a copy of the wreath explanation from page 50 for each child and punch a hole in the top corner. Also punch a hole at the top of the wreath. Attach a piece of red yarn through the explanation and the wreath for a hanger. Encourage the children to share the explanation with their friends and family members.

Candle Pattern

Meaning of the Wreath

A wreath is round and reminds us of God. God is Eternal (I Timothy 1:17), with no beginning nor ending.

The candle reminds us that Christ is the Light of the World (John 3:19), so we too, are to let our lights shine (Matthew 5:16).

Green represents life and hope, and Jesus is the hope of the world (Joel 3:16b).

Red berries remind us that the Lord Jesus died on the cross and shed His blood so that our sins would be forgiven.

The white bow reminds us that Jesus has forgiven (or cleansed) us of our sins so that we may have life eternal.

42 Christmas
Christmas Plan-Ahead Program

OBJECTIVE: To help children visualize the Christmas story and to make it more meaningful to them

Appropriate for ages 3 to 12

"And she brought forth her firstborn Son, and wrapped Him in swaddling clothes, and laid Him in a manger."
— Luke 2:7

Christmas programs are often hectic to produce when December arrives and the participants never get to "see" the program. In order to help lessen the rush of the Season, prepare for the Christmas program ahead of time by taking slides.

Early in the fall take your children and their costumes out into the country to a farm (hopefully you will have made arrangements with a farmer to do this). Have the children pose in costumes depicting the various scenes of the Christmas story. There can be shepherds in the field with real sheep, Joseph leading a donkey carrying Mary or the two of them walking down a dirt road, angels and shepherds kneeling in the straw around Mary and Baby Jesus. Be sure that all the children get to be in one of the pictures. Take slides of each scene from different angles so that you will have several to choose from to best present the story.

As soon as the slides are developed, let the children help determine which ones to use for the program. Then have the children record the Christmas story narrative and several Christmas hymns to accompany the story. Now when the day arrives for the program presentation, the children can sit with their families and friends and see themselves portraying the birth of Jesus.

Christmas
Christmas Tree Puzzle

OBJECTIVE: To help children remember the Christmas story

Appropriate for ages 8 to 12

"For unto you is born this day in the city of David a Saviour, which is Christ the Lord."
— Luke 2:11

Duplicate the Christmas tree puzzle below so that each child has a copy. The children may use their Bibles to help fill in the blanks correctly. Encourage the children to take the puzzles home and, using the words they found, tell the story of Christmas to their family and friends.

Answers: *1. so, 2. God, 3. Mary, 4. Jesus, 5. manger, 6. tidings, 7. heavenly, 8. shepherds, 9. Bethlehem*

1. This Child was born because God _____ loved the world. — John 3:16

2. His father was _____ . — John 3:16

3. His mother was _____.
— Luke 2:5, 7

4. His name was _____.
— Matthew 1:21

5. His bed was a _____.
— Luke 2:7

6. The angels brought _____.
— Luke 2:10

7. The angels who announced His birth were _____. — Luke 2:13

8. The first ones to hear of His birth were _____.
— Luke 2:8-11

9. The town where He was born was _____.
— Luke 2:4, 11

CHRISTMAS

44 Christmas
Little Children's Tree

OBJECTIVE: To make the Christmas story meaningful to small children by encouraging participation

Appropriate for ages 3 to 5

"We have seen His star in the east, and are come to worship Him."
— Matthew 2:2

Here's a Christmas tree idea for your very small children. From green felt, cut the outline of a tree approximately 30 inches high. Cut ornament shapes such as a manger, an angel, a star, a camel, etc., from pieces of brightly colored felt. Mount the tree on a large flannel board or on the wall low enough for the children to reach.

Let the children put the ornaments on the tree as you tell the Christmas story. Try to relate a part of the story for each ornament. Expect the children to add and remove the ornaments again and again as they get the tree ready for Jesus' birthday.

45 Christmas
Christmas Fun

OBJECTIVE: To show children that they can celebrate with friends and can share the joy of Christmas

Appropriate for ages 6 to 12

"Glory to God in the highest, and on earth peace, good will toward men."
— Luke 2:14

The celebration of Christmas has become so secularized that children often have difficulty centering their thoughts on Jesus and His birth. A Sunday school party will provide a meaningful time of celebration and sharing of the Christmas message. Instead of bringing gifts to exchange with each other, ask each child to bring a gift that can be given to a child in a needy family or children's home. Play games, have refreshments, and include a time of devotions during your party. The children could go Christmas caroling around the neighborhood and then return to the party for refreshments. Following are some suggested games.

Preparing the Christmas Dinner. In planning this feast remember that the cook is fussy and does not like P's. Have the players take turns naming something to have for dinner. Anyone who names a food containing the letter P is out. See how many are still in the game after a given time.

Christmas Story Scramble. Type the Christmas story from Luke 2:1-12 (double spaced) on a sheet of paper, omitting verse numbers. Cut the story line by line into as many pieces as there are children. Each one should have a phrase or part of a verse.

Scramble the typed verses in a box and let each child draw one out. The object of the game is to put the verses into the correct order. Give the children time to arrange themselves in order according to the verse or phrase they have, then ask

them to read the story in the proper order.

Balloon Pop. Make a list of basic questions about the Christmas story, with a few fun questions mixed in. Write each question on a slip of paper and insert it in a balloon. Blow up the balloons and tie them around the room. The children take turns finding a balloon, popping it, and answering the question. This will not only liven up the party, but will help you to know where the children are in their knowledge of the Christmas story. The other children will be the judges as to the correctness of the answers.

Snowball Race. Make snowballs out of cotton (about 2-3 inches in diameter). have the children line up side by side. They then put the cotton snowballs on their heads, put their hands behind their back, and see who can get to a designated goal without losing their snowball.

Birthdays

Birthdays are an excellent time to emphasize that each child was created in a special way by God. They are also a good opportunity to reaffirm each child's self-worth and to thank God for the blessings He has given during the past year.

Children's birthdays can be celebrated as they occur during the year or with one large celebration once or twice a year to honor everyone.

46 Birthday
Happy Birthday!

OBJECTIVE: To promote a feeling of self-worth for children

Appropriate for ages 6 to 12

"Oh that men would praise the Lord for His goodness, and for His wonderful works to the children of men!"
— Psalm 107:15

Prepare a large envelope which reads on the outside, "Happy Birthday from All of Us." During pre-session time have the children make cards for the child who has a birthday during the coming week. Put all the cards in the big envelope. This can be delivered to the child's home on the day of his birthday.

Small children like and need to have their birthdays remembered by their teachers. Each Sunday school teacher should keep a record of birthdates for their students and send a birthday card with a personal note to them. How excited the children will be to receive a special note on their birthday.

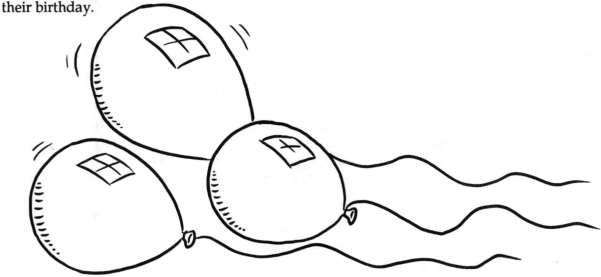

The Seasons — Summer, Fall, Winter, Spring

Devote time to celebrating the various seasons and discussing the wonder of God's creation at different times of year. Learning about the seasons will help children understand that God makes all kinds of weather and that He alone controls it (Genesis 8:22).

47 Summer (June-August)
Summer Clean-Up Picnic

OBJECTIVE: To help children learn several ways to spend the summer hours by helping others

Appropriate for ages 3 to 12

"He that gathereth in summer is a wise son."
— Proverbs 10:5

Plan a summer clean-up picnic for your children. Have them meet together on a Saturday or a weekday morning. Arrange for them to bring a sack lunch or provide a picnic lunch for them. Let them help clean up the Sunday school classrooms or church building and grounds. They can sort out left-over take-home papers for use in the Resource Center, wash windows, dust furniture, help put up new bulletin boards, etc.

Plan to work hard for at least one hour. Then go to a park to play. Prepare a short devotional time following lunch. Thank each child and award him with a certificate.

_____
(Child's Name)

helped clean up our church
on _____.
(Date)

Thanks for your help!

_____
(Teacher or Pastor)

48 Fall (Sept.-Nov.) Fall Mobile

OBJECTIVE: That children will begin to appreciate the change in seasons that signals the harvest

Appropriate for ages 3 to 9

"To every thing there is a season."
— Ecclesiastes 3:1

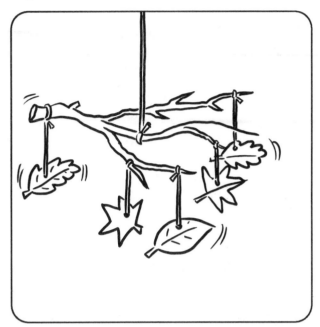

The change in seasons from the warmth of summer to the coolness of fall brings nature projects to mind. The leaves turn many wonderful colors and fall to the ground. Have your children collect some of these leaves to pin on your fall bulletin board for a colorful border.

Bring a small branch to class and tie a string to it so you can hang it for a mobile. Use the leaf patterns below and on page 58 for the children to trace onto construction paper. Let the children cut leaves of various fall colors. Tie these leaves to the branch with thread so they hang at different lengths.

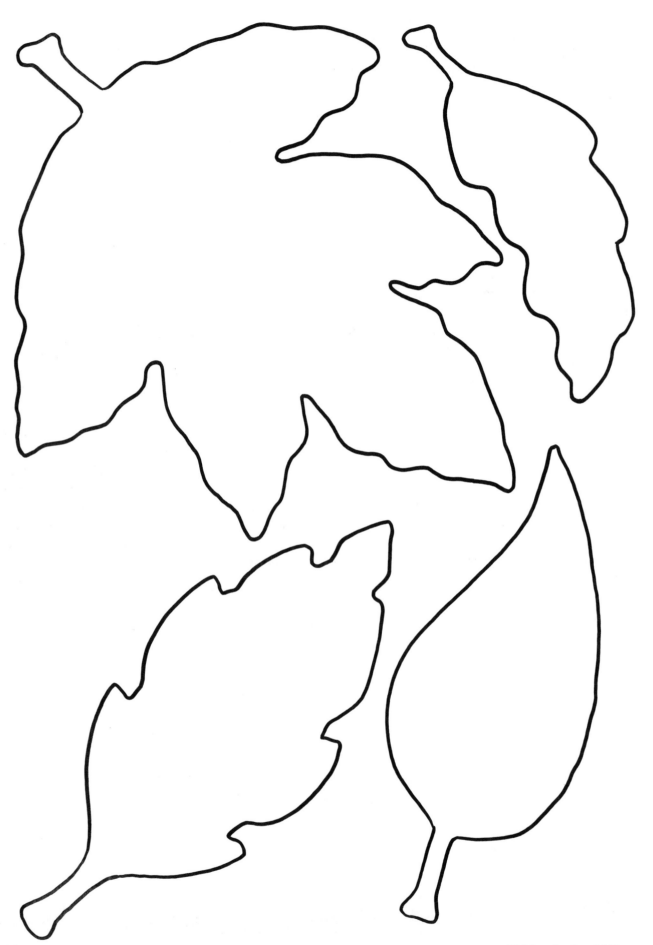

49 Winter (Dec.-Feb.)
Snowy Landscape Picture

OBJECTIVE: To help children appreciate the beauty of the winter season God gave us

Appropriate for ages 3 to 9

"He has made everything beautiful in its time."
— Ecclesiastes 3:11 (NIV)

When winter arrives we begin to think of snow. How wonderful God is that He can make millions and billions of snowflakes and not have any of them like any other. Just like He made us, each one is uniquely different and very special. When we put the snowflakes together we can make interesting and beautiful things, and when we get together with other children of God we are interesting and beautiful, too.

Let the boys and girls think about how beautiful and special they are as they make a snow picture. Bring pictures of snow and snowflakes falling for those children who may not have seen snow before.

Have the children draw and color a snow scene of a park or farm or even their own house and yard on a piece of blue construction paper. Perhaps there will be a snowman standing playfully in the yard. Duplicate a memory verse for each child to cut out and glue on the construction paper.

Mix ½-cup detergent (soap) flakes with a little water, whipping it until you get a mixture like whipped cream. Let the children spread this mixture on their pictures with craft or ice cream sticks. The snow can be on the trees, roof, ground and on the snowman, of course. Set the pictures aside to dry before the children take them home.

> **"He has made everything beautiful in its time."**
> **— Ecclesiastes 3:11 (NIV)**

50 Spring (March-May) Spring Fling

OBJECTIVE: To help children appreciate God's plan for new life

Appropriate for ages 3 to 12

"This is the day which the LORD hath made; we will rejoice and be glad in it."
— Psalm 118:24

The first month of Spring, March, is a windy month and a wonderful time for children to make and fly kites. Outdoors, they can enjoy the new life that is bursting forth from the thawing ground and the budding trees. Let the children bring kites to put together and fly. After the kites have been flown, bring the children inside for a Spring party.

Provide plastic sandwich bags or plastic wrap, flower-shaped cookies (at least two per child), plastic knives, candy sprinkles, and several colors of frosting. Let the children decorate their flowers, eat one, and take one home. Following are some appropriate games.

Drop the Dandelion. Make a dandelion or any other spring flower out of construction paper. Play the game as you would play Drop the Handkerchief. Children enjoy familiar games and will like the new idea of dropping a flower. As the children stand in a circle, give one child the dandelion. He runs around the outside of the circle and drops the flower behind someone. That per-

son picks up the flower and chases the first person until he catches him or until that person reaches the empty space in the line.

Umbrella Toss. Let each child have a turn at trying to toss five jelly beans into an open umbrella. Have the children stand four feet from the umbrella. See who can get the most jelly beans into the umbrella.

Vacation Time

Help children stay in touch with your church program while they are on vacation. Even when they are not able to attend your church, they can be reminded that God is with them, and they can be encouraged to read their take-home papers. When they return, showing interest in what they did during their vacation will make them feel very special.

51 Vacation Time
My Travel Book

OBJECTIVE: To help the children stay close to God during their vacations from Sunday school

Appropriate for ages 6 to 12

"Keep yourselves in the love of God."
— Jude 21

Travel books can become an effective bridge between vacationing children and the Sunday school. Even shy pupils are usually ready to share unique experiences of a trip or a vacation.

Make the books by typing or printing one entry suggestion on each page, allowing plenty of room for the student to write or draw. Make six to eight pages total. Duplicate enough pages for each child to have one. Possible entries are:

I left on my trip at ___ o'clock, on _____ (day). I felt _____ . I traveled on a _____ (car, boat, airplane, train). Here is a picture of what I first saw.
    OR
I began my vacation on _____ (day). I felt _____ . Here is a picture of the first thing I did.
    The funniest thing that happened to me so far was _____ .
    This is a picture postcard of something I found interesting.
    Today we visited _____ .
    We have some interesting souvenirs. I found or bought _____ .

Place the pages into colorful binders or staple a construction paper cover over them to make a travel book for each child. Take-home papers for the Sundays that the child will be away also may be included in the travel book. They will provide good reading materials for the how-much longer-till-we-get-there? times. On the Sunday before his departure, present the book to the student and have a brief prayer for him.

Reserve one Sunday early in the fall for an Around the World in 90 Days theme. Feature interviews, displays, and the completed travel books. Lead into a time of expressing praise and appreciation to God for the opportunities for seeing His creation and for His loving care and protection while traveling.

For those students who will be staying home during vacation, provide a similar book for them to keep track of interesting things they have done at home. No one should be left out of the fun of sharing their summer vacation.

Year 'Round

Teach children that God is with them all year by giving them many opporutunities to celebrate Him and His Son, Jesus. As they learn Christ-centered ways to celebrate the holidays, children will discover new opportunities to share the gospel all year 'round.

52 Year 'Round
Make It Through the Year Game

OBJECTIVE: To encourage children to observe and celebrate special times

Appropriate for ages 6 to 12

"There is a time for everything."
—Ecclesiastes 3:1 (NIV)

Bring buttons or cut small squares of different colors of paper and fold them in half for markers. Duplicate the patterns below and on page 63 and 64. Mount the game board on the inside of a manila file folder. Mount the directions on the other side of the folder and staple a plastic sandwich bag to that side to hold the cards and markers. Mount the spinner on poster board, cut it out, and loosely attach it to the wheel with a brass paper fastener. Place a piece of tape over the fastener to prevent scratching.

Cut page 64 in half and glue each half onto a different bright color of poster board or construction paper. Cut out the cards and place them on the game board in the appropriate piles. Make enough games for every four or five children to have one. Let older children make their own. Provide crayons or markers for decorating.

Spinner

Game Directions

Play starts on New Year's Day, so all markers begin on that square. Spin to see who begins. Each player spins in turn to determine how far to move his marker. Each player must follow the directions on the square on which he lands or stay where he lands until his next turn.

Players take a Special Day Card or Season Card as indicated and follow the directions on the card to move back or forward. How long will it take you to get through the year?

Make It Through the Year Game • Make It Through the Year Game • Make It Through the Year Game

Special Day Cards

Season Cards

Spinner numbers: 8, 1, 2, 3, 4, 5, 6, 7

		Fall Begins Find a leftover firecracker. Go back 2.	Take a Special Day Card	Independence Day (Fourth of July)	
Columbus Day	Labor Day				Summer Begins

Harvest Festival — Father's Day

Thanksgiving — Memorial Day

Take a Season Card — Mother's Day Remembered Mom. Go ahead 2.

Advent begins Go ahead to Christmas. — Take a Season Card

Hanukkah — Easter

Winter begins — Palm Sunday

FINISH Christmas — Spring begins Forgot to send a Valentine to a teacher. Go back 2.

START New Year's Day →	Epiphany	Take a Special Day Card	Presidents' Day	Valentine's Day	St. Patrick's Day

SEASON Spring has sprung. Go ahead 4.	**SEASON** Fall leaves fall. Go back 2.	**SPECIAL DAY** Send Valentine's Cards. Go ahead 2.	**SPECIAL DAY** Rested on Labor Day. Go back 2.
SEASON Summer slump. Go back 3.	**SEASON** Winter snow blows. Go back 2.	**SPECIAL DAY** Didn't wear green on St. Patrick's. Go back 3.	**SPECIAL DAY** Sailed on a ship on Columbus Day. Go ahead 2.
SEASON Fall's back. Go back 4.	**SEASON** Spring rains. Go back 2.	**SPECIAL DAY** Took a friend to church on Easter. Go ahead 4.	**SPECIAL DAY** Didn't invite friends to a Fall Festival. Go back 2.
SEASON Winter chills. Go back 3.	**SEASON** Summer vacation. Go ahead 4.	**SPECIAL DAY** Planted a tree on Arbor Day. Go ahead 2.	**SPECIAL DAY** Thanked God on Thanksgiving. Go ahead 4.
SEASON Spring flowers bloom. Go ahead 3.	**SEASON** Fall harvest. Go ahead 4.	**SPECIAL DAY** Forgot to put up a flag on July 4th. Go back 4.	**SPECIAL DAY** Wished Jewish friends Happy Hanukkah. Go ahead 2.
SEASON Summer sun shines. Go ahead 2.	**SEASON** Winter wonderland. Go ahead 2.	**SPECIAL DAY** Didn't help rake fall leaves. Go back 2.	**SPECIAL DAY** Said Happy Birthday to Jesus on Christmas. Go ahead 4.